DEMON POSSESSION

DEMON DELIVERANCE

FALSE PROPHETS

DR. ERNEST S. MARTIN

ISBN 979-8-88751-870-1 (paperback)
ISBN 979-8-88751-871-8 (digital)

Christian Faith Publishing
832 Park Avenue
Meadville, PA 16335
www.christianfaithpublishing.com

This manuscript is a portion of sermons on demon possession, demon deliverance, and false prophets preached by Dr. Ernest S. Martin, DVM.

Scripture passages are King James Version of the Bible.

The cover page is a photograph of a fire taken by Dr. Ernest S. Martin.

Printed in the United States of America

Second Thessalonians 1:8 says,

> In Flaming fire taking vengeance on them that know not God and that obey not the gospel of our Lord Jesus Christ.

Revelation 20:10–15 says,

> And the devil that deceived them was cast into the lake of fire and brimstone, where the beast and the false prophet are, and shall be tormented day and night for ever and ever. And I saw a great white throne, and him that sat on it, from whose face the earth and the heaven fled away; and there was found no place for them.
>
> And I saw the dead, small and great stand before God; and the books were opened: and another book was opened, which is the book of life: and the dead were judged out of those things which were written in the books, according to their works. And the sea gave up the dead which were in it; and death and hell delivered up the dead which were in them: and they were judged every man according to their works. And death and hell were cast into the lake of fire. This is the second death. And whosoever was not found written in the book of life was cast into the lake of fire.

INTRODUCTION

During the forty-two years that I have been saved, I have seen many doctrines come and go on demon powers and demon spirits. The doctrines vary all the way from those that do not believe that Satan is anything more than a picture that we've seen of the devil in a red suit with horns and a pitchfork. These people don't believe that Satan has any power, and they laugh at anyone that believes that Satan is real.

From that view, other doctrines vary all the way to people who believe that everything they do is caused by Satan and that they are not in control of their own lives. In other words, "The devil made me do it." There are many teachings on demon deliverance that have much and great error. I pray that with guidance from the Holy Spirit and God, we may look at the Word of God and come up with the truth.

On August 21, 1970, I came to realize that I did not know Jesus Christ as my Lord and Savior. I had spent five years of my life believing that I was a Christian and believing that I was serving God. I had met God in an experience similar to Paul's on the road to Damascus when he revealed himself to me in a barn while I was attending veterinary school. At that time, I was an atheist. I was seeking and searching for the truth, and God revealed himself to me.

But on August 21, 1970, I realized that I had never invited Jesus Christ into my heart to be my Lord and Savior. That night, I told God that I would go anyplace, I would do anything, and I would speak any words he asked me to speak. So that weekend, my journey as a born-again believer began as I started to serve and follow God. That night, God gave me a scripture.

John 14:12 says:

> Verily, verily, I say unto you, He that believeth on me, the works that I do shall he do also; and greater works than these shall he do; because I go unto my Father.

I believed that if God could save me that the works Jesus did he could do through me by his Holy Spirit. One of the areas that Jesus did works was demon deliverance. You must understand that at this point, I knew nothing about demon powers and demon deliverance, but I was willing to trust Jesus and learn as the Holy Spirit taught me. I hope to take these experiences with the Word of God to share what I believe the Bible teaches on deliverance and demon-possession.

A few months after I received Jesus Christ as my Lord and Savior, I came to realize that my righteousness was as filthy rags (Isaiah 64:6).

Ephesians 6:18 says:

> Praying always with all prayer and supplication in the Spirit, and watching thereunto with all perseverance and supplication for all saints.

This verse speaks of praying in the spirit. I had never been in a Pentecostal church, and I had never heard anyone pray in tongues. But, one night, as I was sitting on my bed, I asked God how to pray in the spirit. I felt a welling up within me, and I began to speak in another language that I did not know. At the time, I did not know what had happened to me. But the next day, a spirit-filled Jewish believer, who was an evangelist, was sharing with my partner about the baptism of the Holy Spirit. I realized that God had baptized me with his Holy Spirit. After I had received the Holy Spirit, I found a new power to love others that I couldn't love before.

I came home from church and to my wife, who was pregnant with our second child and was running a high fever. We were concerned for the child because the fever was so high, and the doctors were unable to bring it under control. I asked my wife if she believed God could heal her, and she said, "Yes, God can heal."

"I mean, do you really believe that God can heal you?" was my reply. I told her I was going to pray for her as I was led by the Holy Spirit. I rebuked the spirit of infirmity. I felt the spirit of infirmity with the heat and fever coming upon me. She was well. I told the spirit of infirmity in Jesus' name that he must leave me and leave the household. Then he was gone.

Luke 13:10–17 says:

> And he was teaching in one of the synagogues on the sabbath. And, behold, there was a woman which had a spirit of infirmity eighteen years, and was bowed together, and could in no wise lift up herself. And when Jesus saw her, he called her to him, and said unto her, Woman, thou art loosed from thine infirmity. And he laid his hands on her: and immediately she was made straight, and glorified God. And the ruler of the synagogue answered with indignation, because that Jesus had healed on the sabbath day, and said unto the people, There are six days in which men ought to work: in them therefore come and be healed, and not on the sabbath day. The Lord then answered him, and said, Thou hypocrite, doth not each one of you on the sabbath loose his ox or his ass from the stall, and lead him away to watering? And ought not this woman, being a daughter of Abraham, whom Satan hath bound, lo, these eighteen years, be loosed from this bond on the sabbath day? And when he had said these things, all his adversaries were ashamed: and all the people rejoiced for all the glorious things that were done by him.

As Jesus had cast out the spirit of infirmity from the woman that it bound for eighteen years, so the spirit of infirmity had been cast from our household.

KNOW YOUR ENEMY

Before we take on Satan, we need to know who he is, what his goals are, and how he works.

Isaiah 14:12–17 says:

> How art thou fallen from heaven, O Lucifer, son of the morning! how art thou cut down to the ground, which didst weaken the nations! For thou hast said in thine heart, I will ascend into heaven, I will exalt my throne above the stars of God: I will sit also upon the mount of the congregation, in the sides of the north: I will ascend above the heights of the clouds; I will be like the Most High. Yet thou shalt be brought down to hell, to the sides of the pit. They that see thee shall narrowly look upon thee, and consider thee, saying, Is this the man that made the earth to tremble, that did shake kingdoms; That made the world as a wilderness, and destroyed

the cities thereof; that opened not the house of his prisoners?

We find that Satan is an angel fallen from heaven who is the prince of this world system, is the ruler of this world, and is called Lucifer, the day star. His desire is to be God, to be above God, and to rule. He said that he will be like the Most High God, so he is always going to imitate God in the things that he says and the things that he does. He is going to be as much like God as he can possibly be. He will possess men that are in great places of leadership and will cause the world and the kingdoms to shake. He will destroy nations and cities and kingdoms. He will take his prisoners and lock the door and throw away the keys.

John 8:36 says:

> If the Son therefore shall make you free, ye shall be free indeed.

John 8:44 says:

> Ye are of your father the devil, and the lusts of your father ye will do. He was a murderer from the beginning, and abode not in the truth, because there is no truth in him. When he speaks a lie, he speaks of his own: for he is a liar, and the father of it.

Jesus said that if you are not of the Father, your father is Satan. We find that Satan was a murderer from the beginning and did not abide by the truth because there was no truth in him. When he speaks, he speaks a lie, and he is the father of lies.

First Peter 5:8 says:

> Be sober, be vigilant; because your adversary the devil, as a roaring lion, walketh about, seeking whom he may devour.

The devil is like a roaring lion, going about to devour anything in his path.

Ephesians 2:2–3 says:

> Wherein in time past ye walked according to the course of this world, according to the prince of the power of the air, the spirit that now worketh in the children of disobedience: Among whom also we all had our conversation in times past in the lusts of our flesh, fulfilling the desires of the flesh and of the mind; and were by nature the children of wrath, even as others.

We find that Satan is the prince of the power of the air and works in the children of disobedience. So before we came to Christ, we were under the powers of Satan and walked in the works of the flesh and of the mind.

Luke 13:10–17 says:

And he was teaching in one of the synagogues on the sabbath. And, behold, there was a woman which had a spirit of infirmity eighteen years, and was bowed together, and could in no wise lift up herself. And when Jesus saw her, he called her to him, and said unto her, Woman, thou art loosed from thine infirmity. And he laid his hands on her: and immediately she was made straight, and glorified God. And the ruler of the synagogue answered with indignation, because that Jesus had healed on the sabbath day, and said unto the people, There are six days in which men ought to work: in them therefore come and be healed, and not on the sabbath day. The Lord then answered him, and said, Thou hypocrite, doth not each one of you on the sabbath loose his ox or his ass from the stall, and lead him away to watering? And ought not this woman, being a daughter of Abraham, whom Satan hath bound, lo, these eighteen years, be loosed from this bond on the sabbath day? And when he had said these things, all his adversaries were ashamed: and all the people rejoiced for all the glorious things that were done by him.

We find that the spirit of infirmity that could affect the flesh was another means by which Satan harmed and injured mankind.

First Timothy 4:1–4 says:

> Now the Spirit speaketh expressly, that in the latter times some shall depart from the faith, giving heed to seducing spirits, and doctrines of devils; Speaking lies in hypocrisy; having their conscience seared with a hot iron; Forbidding to marry, and commanding to abstain from meats, which God hath created to be received with thanksgiving of them which believe and know the truth. For every creature of God is good, and nothing to be refused, if it be received with thanksgiving.

Satan is a seducing spirit that will draw people away from the truth.

Revelation 20:10 says:

> And the devil that deceived them was cast into the lake of fire and brimstone, where the beast and the false prophet are, and shall be tormented day and night for ever and ever.

The destiny of Satan is to be the lake of fire.

There are three spirits that we need to deal with in our lives; one is the Holy Spirit, one is demonic spirits, and one is our own spirit. The two spirits most difficult to distinguish between are the Holy Spirit and our own spirit. Something that we do not realize is that when you receive Jesus Christ as your Lord and Savior, you now have a spirit that can hear and see the things of God.

Romans 10:17 says:

> So then faith cometh by hearing, and
> hearing by the word of God.

When God speaks to us, he speaks with his Word by the Holy Spirit to our spirit which is now alive. The thing that we need to do is learn to listen to the Spirit so that we may be led by the Spirit and walk in the Spirit. There will be times when you know that you know that it is God, and it is through these experiences that you come to learn to hear the Spirit and to know when the Spirit is speaking and leading you.

Satan took Jesus into the wilderness, and after Jesus had fasted forty days and forty nights, Satan tried to get Jesus to worship him. Satan quoted to Jesus Scriptures, and the Scriptures were usually out of context. Jesus was able to overcome by knowing the truth and quoting back the truth. When people are teaching, God's Word tells us to discern the truth as the Spirit speaks to us. He says in Hebrews chapter 5, "But by reason of use of the Word of God, we will be able to know the truth."

Frist John 4:1–4 says:

> Beloved, believe not every spirit, but try the spirits whether they are of God: because many false prophets are gone out into the world. Hereby know ye the Spirit of God: Every spirit that confesseth that Jesus Christ is come in the flesh is of God: And every spirit that confesseth not that Jesus Christ is come in the flesh is not of God: and this is that spirit of antichrist, whereof ye have heard that it should come; and even now already is it in the world. Ye are of God, little children, and have overcome them: because greater is he that is in you, than he that is in the world.

Believe not every spirit but test the spirits to see if they are of God. I will spend more time on this section of the Scripture later.

BELIEVERS PROTECTION

In First John 4:4, Jesus says:

> Greater is he that is in you than he
> that is in the world.

In Job chapter 1, when Satan comes to God at the throne, God asked him where he had been. Satan said he had been going to and fro in the earth and walking up and down in it. God asked Satan if he had considered his servant Job. Satan said that he couldn't do anything with Job because God had placed a hedge up on him.

Before we take on Satan, we need to know and understand in our spirit that truly greater is he that is in us than he that is in the world. Nothing can happen to us unless God allows. We must know in our own hearts and in our own lives that we are in Jesus Christ and that Satan truly cannot have any effect upon us as long as we are in Christ. The sovereignty of God is the true strength and power for this belief. When we know that we know that God is God, that he is sovereign, and that he only wants the best for us, then if he allows something to happen in our lives, we know that it is for our own good (Romans 8:28).

Ephesians 6:11–20 says:

> Put on the whole armour of God, that ye may be able to stand against the wiles of the devil. For we wrestle not against flesh and blood, but against principalities, against powers, against the rulers of the darkness of this world, against spiritual wickedness in high places. Wherefore take unto you the whole armour of God, that ye may be able to withstand in the evil day, and having done all, to stand. Stand therefore, having your loins girt about with truth, and having on the breastplate of righteousness; And your feet shod with the preparation of the gospel of peace; Above all, taking the shield of faith, herewith ye shall be able to quench all the fiery darts of the wicked. And take the helmet of salvation, and the sword of the Spirit, which is the word of God: Praying always with all prayer and supplication in the Spirit, and watching thereunto with all perseverance and supplication for all saints; And for me, that utterance may be given unto me, that I may open my mouth boldly, to make known the mystery of the gospel, For which I am an ambassador in bonds:

that therein I may speak boldly, as I ought
to speak.

God tells us to put on the whole armor of God and
to take a stand. When we are in the armor of God, we can
withstand all the powers of hell that Satan can muster up
because truly greater is he that is in us than he that is in the
world. God is the one that created the world and controls
the world.

Revelation 12:11 says:

> And they overcame him by the blood
> of the Lamb, and by the word of their
> testimony; and they loved not their lives
> unto the death.

I believe this verse is the most important Scripture that
we must understand in order to take on Satan. The only
hold that Satan really has on us is death. It's an extremely
powerful hold that can bring the greatest fear.

First Peter 5:8–9 says:

> Be sober, be vigilant; because your
> adversary the devil, as a roaring lion,
> walketh about, seeking whom he may
> devour: Whom resist stedfast in the faith,
> knowing that the same afflictions are
> accomplished in your brethren that are in
> the world.

James 4:7 says:

> Submit yourselves therefore to God.
> Resist the devil, and he will flee from you.

Resist the devil. I see and hear people on a regular basis that are going around and saying, "I bind you in Jesus' name, I bind you in Jesus' name, I bind you in Jesus' name" or "I plead the blood, I plead the blood, I plead the blood." Satan has their attention and is preoccupying them. When God says resist the devil, I discovered the best way to resist him is to ignore him. Because you already know that greater is he that is in you than he that is in the world, he can have no effect upon your life, other than to try to distract you from the truth of the power of God's Word. So if you ignore him, after a while, he will go to fresher and greener pastures to find somebody that will give him attention.

Now I am going to relate some personal testimonies of how God brought scriptural truths into my life so that he could use me. I had not been saved but a few months and baptized with the Holy Spirit probably not more than a couple of months. I was driving to work one morning when Satan came to me and said, "I'm going to take everything that you have—your home, your wife, your children, and your practice."

I'm a veterinarian. Satan began to deal with me that everything I had was going to be taken and I would have nothing left. And, eventually, he would take my life. I would like to tell you that I rose up in great faith and rebuked him and walked in great victory, but that was not the case.

Instead, I was overwhelmed, deeply depressed, frightened, and I was in complete fear. I didn't understand what God was doing and what was going on. But as I began to seek God and look at his Word, I began to sort things out after about the third day. I started to realize that if my wife and my boys were to be taken from me, they would go to heaven and have no more suffering. They would be in God's total peace and harmony in love.

We as Christians should look forward to going home to be with him. That began to give me rest. I realized that if I lost my building and my practice and my home, Satan could take my material things, but he could not touch my life. Paul said for me to live is Christ, but to die is gain. I realized that Satan could not take my life unless God allowed it, and if he allowed it, it would actually be victory for me because I would be at home with the Lord. Then I really began to understand that they loved not their lives unto death. Oh death, where is your sting?

On the cross, Christ defeated death and was resurrected. Through his death and resurrection, we have defeated death. I'd like to be able to tell you that this was so deeply burned into my heart that I never feared death or Satan again, but there was more to come. That night, as I sat on the sofa, thinking of God and what he had shown me, suddenly there was a vision of a mass of demons that were coming at me in hordes. They were trying to attack, but there was a shield right in front of my face. They kept hitting the shield and bouncing off and bouncing back. The more they hit, the angrier they became and the more they continued to charge.

After this vision, I began to see the reality of the Scripture that greater is he that is in you than he that is in the world. As in Job, there was a protection of a hedge that God placed around me, and Satan couldn't do anything about it, even though demons continued to attack. Finally, I said, "Lord it's enough. I've seen it."

God didn't answer, and the demons kept coming and coming while they were getting angrier and angrier. God finally began to speak to me that when Jesus sent out his disciples, he gave them power over the spirits.

Luke 9:1 says:

> Then he called his twelve disciples together, and gave them power and author-ity over all devils, and to cure diseases.

Luke 10:18–20 says:

> And he said unto them, I beheld Satan as lightning fall from heaven. Behold, I give unto you power to tread on serpents and scorpions, and over all the power of the enemy: and nothing shall by any means hurt you. Notwithstanding in this rejoice not, that the spirits are subject unto you; but rather rejoice, because your names are written in heaven.

He had given me power in the name of Jesus to rebuke them. I rebuked them in the name of Jesus and told them that they had to be gone. The spirits immediately turned and began to flee, but they were looking back, like an angry, vicious dog with his tail tucked between his legs and his mouth open, growling, and looking back as though he had just been whipped.

The one other thing we need to realize is that God took down the hedge off Job and let Satan take everything he had and attack his flesh, but he was not allowed to take his life. Job went through a very, very difficult and struggling time, but he came to know God in a way that he had not known him. That night, I went to bed and began to dream. The first time, Satan came to me and said that he was going to get me. He came in long dark black hair, and he held out a gun and said, "I'm going to kill you."

I rebuked him in Jesus' name and told him to be gone. Then, as I was walking down the street, he came to me again in a different disguise and said that he was going to kill me. I said, "In the name of Jesus I rebuke you."

Suddenly I was beginning to well up with pride and confidence that I could take on Satan in any form or way. I could handle him because in the name of Jesus, he had to be gone. I continued to dream that I needed a haircut. I went to the barbershop, but my regular barber was not there. I sat in the chair, and he started to cut my hair. Suddenly, the barber pulled out a straight razor and was ready to cut my throat. Then I recognized it was Satan. I rebuked him in the name of Jesus. Fear began to creep in. I feared what was going to happen, knowing that Satan sometimes would come in like a roaring lion and at other times like a fox.

I wasn't always going to be able to see him and recognize him. Also, I realized that I could not trust myself.

As we saw in the Scriptures, Satan is deceptive. The Scripture says to take heed if you think you stand, lest you fall. When we think we are in our strength, we may be at our greatest weakness. In this part of the dream, I began to get frightened. Satan had said, "I'm going to kill you." But now I didn't know what he looked like, I didn't know what disguise he would use, and I did not know what instrument he was going to use to kill me. I ran into this huge room filled with large boxes that one could hide behind. I ran and I ran, and he kept chasing me until, finally, I was totally exhausted.

I stopped and cried out to God. The Lord gave me the Scripture that they overcame him by the blood of the Lamb, by the word of their testimonies, and they loved not their lives unto death. I just stopped and said, "Satan, you can destroy this flesh, but you cannot destroy me because my name is written in the book of life, and I will go straight home to be with Jesus. So if you want to kill me, do it."

At that moment, I awoke. I was completely exhausted, and the bed was covered in sweat. I was lying in what seemed to be a pool of water. It was my own sweat. I had literally been running in bed. Then, suddenly, I saw Satan standing in the clothes closet, and he said again that he was going to kill me. Fear gripped me all over again. As I faced the reality that he was standing there, watching all of this, and ready to pounce on me, I looked at him and told Satan to be gone because if he killed me, I would go home to be with Jesus. At that moment, total and complete peace came upon me because I realized deep in my spirit that Satan no longer had a hold on me, and death was not to be feared. Because I no longer feared Satan, I was later able to meet with the high priest of the Church of Satan of the Southwest District.

I don't consider myself a spiritual giant but just an ordinary person. If God can take me, an ordinary person, and teach me and use me, he can use each and every one that is open, willing, and ready to be of use to him. These are some of the things that I hope will encourage and inspire each person that reads this book: to be open to the things of God, to be available, to be used, and to realize that God is no respecter of persons. He will use anyone that wants to be used.

Jesus himself, when he was selecting disciples, did not go out and select the spiritual leaders but primarily fishermen and ordinary men that he might use them to further his kingdom. One of the other things that I think is important is to protect people, especially the innocent ones, who may or may not have come to Christ. I have changed some of the names and circumstances to protect them, but in no way will it change what God has done, the reality of walking with him, or the context of what has happened.

DEMONS OF INFIRMITY

Not too long after I received Christ and when God began to work in my life, I taught a Bible study in our home, both on Tuesday nights and on Friday nights. The Friday night study was reserved for young men who had surrendered to the ministry that wanted to help solve the problems in the lives of others. As we continued to meet on Friday nights, we started going out to a parking lot in Dallas where the young people, as well as many older people, gathered on Friday night to do drugs, drink alcohol, and do all types of things.

As we went out the first night to witness, there were two young ladies that came and received Jesus Christ as their Lord and Savior. They started attending the church that we attended. One day, one of these high school girls approached me. She stated that she had a nephew, who was around seven or eight months of age, who had epileptic seizures. They had taken her nephew to two or three different doctors and to a specialist, but they were unable to find the right medication to give the child to stop the seizures. As she shared this with me, she asked if I would pray for him. I said that I would pray for him. That evening, as I was studying the Word of God and praying, God turned me to Mark.

Mark 9:14–29 says:

> And when he came to his disciples, he saw a great multitude about them, and the scribes questioning with them. And straightway all the people, when they beheld him, were greatly amazed, and running to him saluted him. And he asked the scribes, What question ye with them? And one of the multitude answered and said, Master, I have brought unto thee my son, which hath a dumb spirit; And wheresoever he taketh him, he teareth him: and he foameth, and gnasheth with his teeth, and pineth away: and I spake to thy disciples that they should cast him out; and they could not. He answereth him, and saith, O faithless generation, how long shall I be with you? how long shall I suffer you? bring him unto me. And they brought him unto him: and when he saw him, straightway the spirit tare him; and he fell on the ground, and wallowed foaming. And he asked his father, How long is it ago since this came unto him? And he said, Of a child. And ofttimes it hath cast him into the fire, and into the waters, to destroy

him: but if thou canst do any thing, have compassion on us, and help us. Jesus said unto him, If thou canst believe, all things are possible to him that believeth. And straightway the father of the child cried out, and said with tears, Lord, I believe; help thou mine unbelief. When Jesus saw that the people came running together, he rebuked the foul spirit, saying unto him, Thou dumb and deaf spirit, I charge thee, come out of him, and enter no more into him. And the spirit cried, and rent him sore, and came out of him: and he was as one dead; insomuch that many said, He is dead. But Jesus took him by the hand, and lifted him up; and he arose. And when he was come into the house, his disciples asked him privately, Why could not we cast him out? And he said unto them, This kind can come forth by nothing, but by prayer and fasting.

The father had brought a young boy that had seizures to the disciples, and they could not heal him. They brought him to Jesus, and Jesus said to the father if he could believe, all things were possible.

The father said, "I believe, but help my unbelief."

Jesus cast the demon out of the young boy, and he appeared dead, but Jesus picked him up by his hand, and he was alive. I wondered how I was going to tell this young lady that her nephew had a demon that was causing the epilepsy. But I knew that I had heard the faith, and I knew that God could heal him if the demon was cast out of him. So when the young lady came to the Bible study the next Tuesday, I opened Mark 9:14–29 and read it to her. And as I did, she came to realize that this was God speaking to her. So I told her to bring her nephew to the house, and we would pray for him.

She brought her nephew to the house, and as I approached him, he began to get really fussy and scream. I reached over, put my hand on his forehead, and commanded that the demon would leave him in Jesus' name and not return. This young child never had another seizure. The doctor said that they must have missed their diagnosis because seizures do not just disappear.

POWER OF SATAN

Matthew 24:24 says:

> For there shall arise false Christs, and
> false prophets, and shall shew great signs
> and wonders; insomuch that, if it were
> possible, they shall deceive the very elect.

I talked earlier about going to the parking lot. We also took the youth choir who sang gospel songs. Then, following the singing, I would preach a salvation message. Afterward, we would stand around, leaning up against cars, and wait for the people to come to us so that we might share Christ. They knew who to come to because we all had Bibles in our hands.

One night, after I had preached, my wife was leaning against a car with the Bible in her hand when a young man approached her. He asked her about forgiveness, walking with God, and serving Christ. He related to her the power that he had to pray for people to be healed and how they were healed. Many other things were going on in his life.

The one big thing that was very troubling was that he was extremely tormented. He said that even at night, he was tormented and couldn't sleep.

So she asked him if he would like to talk to me, and he said he would. She brought him over to me, and I began to visit with him. I realized that he, and even by his own admission, had sold out his life to Satan. Satan had appeared to him and told him that he would give him great powers if he would just serve and walk with him. He related many, many instances where he prayed for people to be healed, and they were healed, and he shared great signs and wonders he said he could perform. He said the power that he had was outstanding. But this power wasn't always used for good; sometimes it was used for evil.

He shared an experience that happened with his best friend. The man became angry with his friend, and he asked Satan to harm him but not destroy him. Within twenty-four hours, his friend was severely injured and suffers even to this day.

Second Corinthians 11:1–15 says:

> Would to God ye could bear with me a little in my folly: and indeed bear with me. For I am jealous over you with godly jealousy: for I have espoused you to one husband, that I may present you as a chaste virgin to Christ. But I fear, lest by any means, as the serpent beguiled Eve through his subtilty, so your minds should be corrupted from the simplicity that is

in Christ. For if he that cometh preacheth another Jesus, whom we have not preached, or if ye receive another spirit, which ye have not received, or another gospel, which ye have not accepted, ye might well bear with him. For I suppose I was not a whit behind the very chiefest apostles. But though I be rude in speech, yet not in knowledge; but we have been thoroughly made manifest among you in all things. Have I committed an offence in abasing myself that ye might be exalted, because I have preached to you the gospel of God freely? I robbed other churches, taking wages of them, to do you service. And when I was present with you, and wanted, I was chargeable to no man: for that which was lacking to me the brethren which came from Macedonia supplied: and in all things I have kept myself from being burdensome unto you, and so will I keep myself. As the truth of Christ is in me, no man shall stop me of this boasting in the regions of Achaia. Wherefore? because I love you not? God knoweth. But what I do, that I will do, that I may cut off occasion from them which desire occasion; that wherein they glory, they may be found even as we. For such are false apostles, deceitful workers, transforming themselves into the apostles of Christ. And no marvel; for Satan himself is transformed into an angel of light. Therefore it is no great thing if his ministers also be transformed as the ministers of righteousness; whose end shall be according to their works.

In this Scripture, Satan is transformed into an angel of light. This young man, as we visited with him, talked about that while he was doing drugs and other things, somehow Satan had come to him as an angel of light, telling him that he would give him great powers if he would commit his life to him. The young man told of many experiences where people had been healed.

I opened the Word of God and shared Christ with him. He was broken and weeping. We asked if he would like to turn his life over to Christ and stop the pain and torment. Our hearts were broken as this young man said that he was tired of being tormented but that he could not give up the great power that he had. He wanted to hang on to the power that he had, so he walked away.

Later that night, in the same parking lot, after I had finished preaching, a man drove up to me in a car. This man had suffered a grave injury. He told that while traveling with his companion, his best friend, they had a heated argument and disagreement. Within twenty-four hours, he was severely injured. This was the man that the other man had prayed about to be harmed. We shared Christ with him. He wasn't ready to receive Christ at that moment, but he knew that Christ was the answer.

This was a tragedy of ignorance. So many people that I was later to meet and will describe in later chapters were young people, and most of them were on drugs. As they were overdosing on that final, potentially fatal trip, the angel of light appeared unto them and said that he would deliver them and save them if they would serve him. He would transform them into ministers of righteousness.

One thing that I think is very important as we look at people who come to Christ is that the Word of God says if you will seek the Lord God with all your heart, he shall be found.

Deuteronomy 4:29 says:

> But if from thence thou shalt seek the Lord thy God, thou shalt find him, if thou seek him with all thy heart and with all thy soul.

John 6:44 says:

> No man can come to me, except the Father which hath sent me draw him: and I will raise him up at the last day.

One of the things I think is so commonly misconceived and is in error is that people believe that they can just wake up someday and come to God or that they can find him in all kinds of strange and weird places. People will take

LSD or other things to try to have a spiritual experience and gain understanding. But God said you must seek him with all your heart in order to find him. You do not find God on drugs or when you're in a drunken stupor. There are many times when people seeking after things that are not of God come to have a relationship with someone that isn't from God.

Deuteronomy 13:5 says:

> And that prophet, or that dreamer of dreams, shall be put to death; because he hath spoken to turn you away from the LORD your God, which brought you out of the land of Egypt, and redeemed you out of the house of bondage, to thrust thee out of the way which the LORD thy God commanded thee to walk in. So shalt thou put the evil away from the midst of thee.

Exodus 20:1–17 says:

> And God spake all these words, saying, I am the LORD thy God, which have brought thee out of the land of Egypt, out of the house of bondage. Thou shalt have no other gods before me. Thou shalt not make unto thee any graven image, or any likeness of any thing that is in heaven above, or that is in the earth beneath, or

that is in the water under the earth: Thou shalt not bow down thyself to them, nor serve them: for I the LORD thy God am a jealous God, visiting the iniquity of the fathers upon the children unto the third and fourth generation of them that hate me; And shewing mercy unto thousands of them that love me, and keep my commandments. Thou shalt not take the name of the LORD thy God in vain; for the LORD will not hold him guiltless that taketh his name in vain. Remember the sabbath day, to keep it holy. Six days shalt thou labour, and do all thy work: But the seventh day is the sabbath of the LORD thy God: in it thou shalt not do any work, thou, nor thy son, nor thy daughter, thy manservant, nor thy maidservant, nor thy cattle, nor thy stranger that is within thy gates: For in six days the LORD made heaven and earth, the sea, and all that in them is, and rested the seventh day: wherefore the LORD blessed the sabbath day, and hallowed it. Honour thy father and thy mother: that thy days may be long upon the land which the LORD thy God giveth thee. Thou shalt not kill. Thou shalt not commit adultery. Thou shalt not steal. Thou shalt not bear false witness against thy neighbour. Thou shalt not covet thy neighbour's house,

thou shalt not covet thy neighbour's wife,
nor his manservant, nor his maidservant,
nor his ox, nor his ass, nor any thing that
is thy neighbour's.

God gave the Ten Commandments to the nation of Israel. He said that since "I am the Lord your God which has brought you out of the land of Egypt, out of the house of bondage, you will have no other gods before me. You shall not make unto you any graven images or likenesses of anything that is in heaven above, or in the earth beneath, or in the water."

What God is clearly saying here is that if you are seeking anything that is idolatrous and that will bring evil, there will be judgment. If you are taking drugs to find peace or to find God, this is an abomination. It is idolatry. And that brings God's judgment to people that do this commonly. They are sometimes seeking after idols and don't realize it.

We should think in our minds about what an idol really is. Jesus Christ came to give us peace. You see, anything that substitutes for what God the Father, God the Son, and God the Holy Spirit can do is idolatry. God is just and said that he curses those who follow idolatry. We can't find God, except we seek after him with all our hearts. The number one place to find God is in the Word of God. The number two place to find God is in the house of God where the Word of truth is preached in holiness and righteousness.

God is not found through drugs. He is not found through seeking self-glory, strength, power, or money. He can be found in his Word when we humble ourselves.

Psalms says the law of the Lord is perfect converting the soul. As we continue to study, we are going to have more and more testimonies of where people were deceived. Many who came to him were made ministers of righteousness, but these people were still not saved. They were walking without the peace that passes all understanding that only Jesus Christ can give. This is a sad thing in men's lives where they are disrupting and hurting their best friends, all because of the powers of darkness.

DEMON-POSSESSED

I received a call late one night somewhere around 11:30 or 12:00 from a young lady that had a cat that was very ill. I met her at my animal hospital, and I examined the cat. It became evident to me that the cat had leukemia. In the process of examining the cat and talking with her, I began to share my conversion on how I received Jesus Christ and what Christ meant to me. As I shared, she wept and opened herself and said to me that she wished that she had what I had. She had tried to pray the sinner's prayer several times, and nothing had happened, and her life did not change.

At that time, I was doing cancer research with Morton Cancer and Wadley Institute. They were using a new drug. It required an IV injection into the cat daily for twenty-eight days. The drug was very effective in reversing leukemia in cats. She came in daily, and God opened the doors for me to share with her. I never forced my opinions on her, never tried to cram the Scriptures down her throat, nor force her to come to Christ. I just ministered to her while working on her cat whose name was Lucifer.

God opened the doors to give her Scriptures. I invited her to go to church with us, and she started going to church where we were attending. She came forward one night as the altar call was given. She sat down with my wife and the pastor's wife. My wife called me over because they were not having any luck in ministering to her. This young lady had tried to commit suicide twenty-five times. She was involved in drugs and had participated in spiritual séances, the Ouija boards, and all types of spiritual demonic activities.

The Lord began to speak to my heart that she was demon-possessed and that she needed to be delivered. I had never prayed for anyone to be delivered. I knew nothing about deliverance and how to pray for someone for deliverance. God told me to invite her to our home the next evening, and she agreed to come. I sat down with her on the sofa, and we visited for a few minutes. Then the Lord told me to go to chapter 1 of Genesis. I wish I could say I was on board, but my reaction was to think that no one leads someone to the Lord reading Genesis 1. We need to stop and set some guidelines as God's Word says what it says. You can argue with the messenger all you want, but God's Word is what you are arguing against. Many false doctrines and traditions have been started by ignoring God's Word and following man's interpretation of the scripture. The Pharisees and priests considered their doctrines and traditions as truth, and they caused multitudes of people to go astray. Then as I opened my Bible, I had her open her Bible to Genesis 1.

Genesis 1:1–27 says:

In the beginning God created the heaven and the earth. And the earth was without form, and void; and darkness was upon the face of the deep. And the Spirit of God moved upon the face of the waters. And God said, Let there be light: and there was light. And God saw the light, that it was good: and God divided the light from the darkness. And God called the light Day, and the darkness he called Night. And the evening and the morning were the first day. And God said, Let there be a firmament in the midst of the waters, and let it divide the waters from the waters. And God made the firmament, and divided the waters which were under the firmament from the waters which were above the firmament: and it was so. And God called the firmament Heaven. And the evening and the morning were the second day. And God said, Let the waters under the heaven be gathered together unto one place, and let the dry land appear: and it was so. And God called the dry land Earth; and the gathering together of the waters called the Seas: and God saw that it was good. And God said, Let the earth bring forth grass, the herb yielding seed, and the fruit tree yielding fruit after his kind, whose seed is in itself, upon the earth: and it was so. And the earth brought forth grass, and herb yielding seed after his kind, and the tree yielding fruit, whose seed was in itself, after his kind: and God saw that it was good. And the evening and the morning were the third day. And God said, Let there be lights in the firmament of the heaven to divide the day from the night; and let them be for signs, and for seasons, and for days, and years: And let them be for lights in the firmament of the heaven to give light upon the earth: and it was so. And God made two great lights; the greater light to rule the day, and the lesser light to rule the night: he made the stars also. And God set them in the firmament of the heaven to give light upon the earth, And to rule over the day and over the night, and to divide the light from the darkness: and God saw that it was good. And the evening and the morning were the fourth day. And God said, Let the waters bring forth abundantly the moving creature that hath life, and fowl that may fly above the earth in the open firmament of heaven. And God created great whales, and every living creature that moveth, which the waters brought forth abundantly, after their kind, and every winged fowl after his kind: and God saw that it was good. And God blessed them, saying, Be fruitful, and multiply, and fill the waters in the seas, and let fowl multiply in the earth. And the evening and the morning were the fifth day. And God said, Let the earth bring forth the living creature after his kind, cattle, and creeping thing, and beast of the earth after his kind: and it was so. And God made the beast of the earth after his kind, and cattle after their kind, and every thing that creepeth upon the earth after his kind: and God saw that it was good. And God said, Let us make man in our image, after our likeness: and let them have dominion over the fish of the sea, and over the fowl of the air, and over the cattle, and over all the earth, and over every creeping thing that creepeth upon the earth. So God created man in his own image, in the image of God created he him; male and female created he them.

As I began to read, I realized that as God described the existence of the earth (it was void and darkness was upon the face of the earth), it also really described a person's life without Christ (that it has no purpose, that it has no direction). There is emptiness, vastness, and darkness. Then the

Scripture says that God moved upon the face of the waters and God said, "Let there be light."

I saw that after each day, God saw that it was good. Then my understanding was open to see something that I had never seen before. God created the first day for the fourth day, the second day for the fifth day, and the third day for the sixth day. On the first day, God created light; and on the fourth day, God created the moon and the sun and the stars. On the second day, God divided the firmament; and on the fifth day, God put the fish and the whales in the sea and the birds in the air. On the third day, God created dry land and vegetation; and on the sixth day, God created animals and man.

When I saw this, I said, "See how God is a God of order. Everything God did was good and orderly and had a purpose and direction."

At that moment, the Holy Spirit began to work upon her life in a powerful way. She literally jumped up off the couch and said, "There is nothing good in my life. There is nothing orderly, and I have been serving and following Satan and did not know it. Satan has controlled of my life for years and years. I don't want him to have control anymore. I want him to leave me alone and I want to come to this peace. I want to come to Jesus Christ."

I walked over to her and told her in her own words to tell Satan that she did not want him in her life anymore and that he must leave. Then she said that she wanted God to save her and to become her Lord and Savior. I asked her if what she truly wanted was that God would become her

Lord and Savior, and she replied, "Yes." She said, "Satan, you'll have no more part in my life."

At that moment, I put my hands upon her, and I commanded that Satan be gone in the name of Jesus. She asked God to forgive her, and she asked Christ to come into her heart. She was gloriously saved, and the peace that passes all understanding, the peace that only God can give, came in and filled her soul. She began to walk with God. She asked that we start a Bible study in our home that would be mainly for drug addicts, hippies, and people like her who were asking what happened to her that so transformed and changed her life. She told them that she had wonderful peace that only Jesus could give.

I would like to tell you that this young lady just walked in glorious harmony and love and victory with power, but she didn't. Something that we noticed, and that she noticed as well, was that when she was with a group of Christians, she had great joy and peace. It seemed like each night as she went home, she was oppressed. She struggled until she was around Christians again, either at the Bible study or the worship service. Finally, God turned me to the book of Acts.

Acts 19:18–20 says:

> And many that believed came, and confessed, and shewed their deeds. Many of them also which used curious arts brought their books together, and burned them before all men: and they counted the price of them, and found it fifty thousand

pieces of silver. So mightily grew the word
of God and prevailed.

In the town of Ephesus, the people who had been
involved in many of the different types of things in the
spiritual world realized that they needed to get rid of the
things that they had used, so they brought these things to
be burned. I asked the young lady if she would like for me
to come to her house and find out why it was so oppressive.
She said she would love for me to come by. So a friend of
mine and I met at her house.

Upon entering the house, I found that she still had
the candles that she burned at séances. We found many
other things that had to deal with the occult, but the one
big thing that we discovered was that there was a picture
hanging on the wall of a Spanish princess who was a spiritualist, probably back in the 1500s or 1600s. This painting
was given to her by one of the people who introduced her
to a spiritualist.

I know that many people have watched a program
called *Bewitched*. In that program, there was a picture on
the wall that I think was of the grandfather, although I'm
not positive. The eyes in that picture followed you around
the room. I can remember as a child watching this while
laughing and thinking, *Oh boy, isn't this far out.* But the first
thing that happened when we went into her house was that
I noticed that the eyes in this painting were glued upon us,
and they started to follow us.

As I walked across the room, the eyes turned and followed me all the way across the room. My friend noticed

this, so without saying anything, he went to one side of the room and sat down. I watched the eyes follow him as he went over to the other side of the room. Then after he sat down, I walked to the other side of the room, and we both watched the eyes turn and follow me across the room. I turned to him, and he turned to me. We looked at each other and both at the same time said, "Did you see what I saw?"

We both said, "Yes."

I've come to learn that sometimes objects that are brought into rooms and into homes have spiritual powers from where they have been and how they were used. This can cause tremendous problems. I am going to share another incident later about how this happened to a young boy in a family and how the powers affected that young man.

I pointed out the painting to this young lady and told her how we had noticed that the eyes followed us. She said she knew that the eyes would follow her and that she had prayed to this person many times. At this time, we read in Acts 19:18–19 that the Ephesians had been involved in the occult. After they received Christ, they brought the books and paraphernalia that they had been using in their occult practices and burned them. We took the things she had been using in spiritualism and burned them in the fireplace. We took the painting and destroyed it. We read Psalms 91 and claimed it for her house.

Psalms 91 says:

He that dwelleth in the secret place of the most High shall abide under the shadow of the Almighty. I will say of the Lord, He is my refuge and my fortress: my God; in him will I trust. Surely he shall deliver thee from the snare of the fowler, and from the noisome pestilence. He shall cover thee with his feathers, and under his wings shalt thou trust: his truth shall be thy shield and buckler. Thou shalt not be afraid for the terror by night; nor for the arrow that flieth by day; Nor for the pestilence that walketh in darkness; nor for the destruction that wasteth at noonday. A thousand shall fall at thy side, and ten thousand at thy right hand; but it shall not come nigh thee. Only with thine eyes shalt thou behold and see the reward of the wicked. Because thou hast made the Lord, which is my refuge, even the most High, thy habitation; There shall no evil befall thee, neither shall any plague come nigh thy dwelling. For he shall give his angels charge over thee, to keep thee in all thy ways. They shall bear thee up in their hands, lest thou dash thy foot against a stone. Thou shalt tread upon the lion and adder: the young lion and the dragon shalt thou trample under feet. Because he hath set his love upon me, therefore will I deliver him: I will set him on high, because he hath known my name. He shall call upon me, and I will answer him: I will be with him in trouble; I will deliver him, and honour him. With long life will I satisfy him, and shew him my salvation.

The doorposts were anointed with oil, and we commanded that Satan and his demonic powers leave the house and not return because the house was now sanctified by God. We saw firsthand the tremendous powers of darkness and how they could have a stronghold on a person's life. Delving into the occult is very, very dangerous. I want to emphasize at this time that many Christians still dress up in costumes and go out on Halloween.

I can remember as a boy growing up, we had carnivals sponsored by the PTA to raise money for the school. There was always somebody that had to be a fortune-teller. Let me tell you that in Deuteronomy 18, God deals with this. People say that it's just a fun thing and that it isn't a horrible thing. It is very dangerous to do things of the occult. God does not honor ignorance. Just like the person who reads horoscopes and says, "I'm a Christian and I don't really believe it." Oh, but we have opened the door. There are so many areas that we open the door.

How many times I've counseled with somebody who played with things related to the occult that led to demon possession. When as a child, they dressed up as a witch to go trick-or-treating or in a carnival they played fortune-tellers, some of the things that they said came true. How many had an Ouija board and played with it as a toy? You can buy these things, including the crazy eight-ball and tarot cards in department and toy stores. These things are idolatry. They are an abomination to God. Ignorance is no excuse. Whatever you do, do not mess with these things because they lead to heartache.

I was teaching a Bible study to couples who were primarily from the North Dallas area. One day, I received a phone call from one of the people who had been coming to the Bible study. She shared some of the things that happened to them because of the Word and the Bible study. After we visited, she mentioned that there was someone she knew whose son was waking up at night. This was a young boy somewhere around ten years of age. He usually woke up somewhere around midnight and became very, very violent when the parents would try to settle him down. We are talking about a young child who could literally pick up the sofa over his head and throw it at his parents.

His parents had recently come to Christ, and their desire was to serve and follow God. I told this woman the child was probably demon-possessed and probably needed to be delivered. So she called the couple and told them that their child was demon-possessed. It didn't take long before I received a phone call from the family of this boy. After I talked with them for a short period of time, they asked me if I would come to their home and pray for their son. They wanted us to come close to the time that he would awaken and do the things that he did each night. So we went over around ten o'clock and shared the Scriptures with the couple.

Mark 5:2–15 says:

> And when he was come out of the ship, immediately there met him out of the tombs a man with an unclean spirit, Who had *his* dwelling among the tombs; and no man could bind him, no, not with chains: Because that he had been often bound with fetters and chains, and the chains had been plucked asunder by him, and the fetters broken in pieces: neither could any *man* tame him. And always, night and day, he was in the mountains, and in the tombs, crying, and cutting himself with stones. But when he saw Jesus afar off, he ran and worshipped him, And cried with a loud voice, and said, What have I to do with thee, Jesus, *thou* Son of the most high God? I adjure thee by God, that thou torment me not. For he said unto him, Come out of the man, *thou* unclean spirit. And he asked him, What *is* thy name? And he answered, saying, My name *is* Legion: for we are many. And he besought him much that he would not send them away out of the country. Now there was there nigh unto the mountains a great herd of swine feeding. And all the

devils besought him, saying, Send us into the swine, that we may enter into them. And forthwith Jesus gave them leave. And the unclean spirits went out, and entered into the swine: and the herd ran violently down a steep place into the sea, (they were about two thousand;) and were choked in the sea. And they that fed the swine fled, and told *it* in the city, and in the country. And they went out to see what it was that was done. And they come to Jesus, and see him that was possessed with the devil, and had the legion, sitting, and clothed, and in his right mind: and they were afraid.

When we walked into the home, we saw a huge tapestry of a Buddhist temple on the wall. We saw many paintings that appeared demonic. Some of these paintings were extremely expensive as this family was a family of wealth. About eleven o'clock that evening, the boy became restless, but he never got up. We continued to talk to the couple about what happened in the book of Acts at Ephesus and how they burned the things that were used to worship in the occult. The family had a large fireplace, and they lit it. Then they started through the home, taking down paintings and many other things that they had in the house before they came to Christ that had spiritual significance and that were not of God. They burned all these things in the fireplace.

I asked them about the tapestry, and they said it was not theirs, that it was on loan from another family. They would return it the next day to the other family. They eliminated a lot of things that probably were not necessary, but if there were any questions, they decided to get rid of them. There was one thing that sat on the fireplace that they had not noticed. It was a ceramic Siamese cat with emerald eyes that came out of one of the Pyramids in Egypt. The Siamese cat was worshipped in Egypt. When I asked them about the Siamese cat, they said it was a gift from her dad to their son. It was the day that the cat was given to their son that he started these violent outbursts at night. The father took the cat out to the driveway and pulverized it with a sledgehammer. Then I cast the demons out of their son. Because the parents were Christians, I prayed that their son would be protected from demons until he could accept Jesus as his savior. Before I prayed for him, he was restless, but then he relaxed and had no more violent episodes. The son had no more outbursts and had peace in a very short time. Later he was led to Christ by his parents.

EMPTY HOUSE

I met a woman that had been going to a charismatic church. She was demon-possessed. The pastor had called her out because God had shown him that she was demon-possessed. He prayed for her deliverance, but she did not receive Jesus Christ as her Savior. This woman now believed that she was the mother of Jesus and that Jesus was her son. She was not able to function as a normal person. She was not mentally ill but was completely controlled by demonic spirits.

This lady was totally nonfunctional, and her life was nothing but torment. In medicine, we have an edict to do no harm. We may not be able to heal an animal or a person, but we do not want to make it worse. This pastor had added to this woman's problems by not explaining that once the demons were gone, she needed to accept Jesus Christ as her Lord and Savior. I wish that I could say that this was the only time that I had seen this.

There was a man who went to a church, and he was demon-possessed. He got up in the middle of the pastor's sermon and began to yell and scream. He took a two-inch leather-bound Bible and ripped it in two as you would rip a sheet of paper. The pastor called him forward, and the man went to the altar. The pastor began to cast out the demons, and the man started to scream and holler and got on the floor and withered like a snake. The pastor cast the demons out of him. The man left the church without receiving Christ.

Several weeks later, another man brought this man to my office and asked me to minister to him. I sat down with the man, started talking to him, and found out that the man had been in the army and had been declared mentally ill. He spent three years in the mental hospital in the army. They were not able to help him or do anything for him, so they gave him a medical discharge from the army. This man was on disability, unable to work or function, and he had been this way for several years.

As I talked with him, I realized in a few minutes that he wasn't the least bit interested in coming to Christ. I told him that he was not interested in coming to Jesus. He said, "You are very perceptive. I serve my own gods, and I don't need yours." So I told him that I was not going to waste my time or his time anymore. He said, "Good."

I asked to pray for him before he left, and he said that he must ask the spirits if it was okay for me to pray for him. I immediately silently bound the spirits of darkness. He looked at me rather strangely because the spirits were not speaking to him. He said this was strange because he was not hearing from his god. He told me he guessed it would be okay for me to pray for him.

Second Corinthians 4:3–6 says:

> But if our gospel be hid, it is hid to them that are lost: In whom the god of this world hath blinded the minds of them which believe not, lest the light of the glorious gospel of Christ, who is the image of God, should shine unto them. For we preach not ourselves, but Christ Jesus the Lord; and ourselves your servants for Jesus' sake. For God, who commanded the light to shine out of darkness, hath shined in our hearts, to give the light of the knowledge of the glory of God in the face of Jesus Christ.

If our gospel is hidden, it is hidden to them who are lost, whom the god of this world, Satan, has blinded their minds that they might not come to the light. So I laid my hands on the man and said, "I bind the spirits in the name of Jesus that they may no longer blind your mind, and I loosen your mind that you might receive the truth of the gospel of Jesus Christ."

When I finished praying, he seemed to be stunned. I gave him the address of the church, and I told him, "When you are ready to seek God with all your heart and receive Christ as your Savior, come to the church."

Six months later, he came to the service, and when the invitation was given, he came forward and said that he wanted to receive Christ. I asked him to have a seat, and when I had finished ministering to the other people, I told him that we would go to the office, and I would pray with him. I took him to the office, opened the Scriptures, and showed him how he could come to Christ. He told me, "I am demon-possessed. I have been possessed for years, and Satan has been my God. I am tired of being tormented by Satan and his demons. I want the peace and joy that you have in your Savior, Jesus Christ."

I told him that in his own words just to tell Satan that he would have to leave, to ask God for his forgiveness, and to invite Jesus Christ into his life. He told Satan to leave. I laid my hands on him and commanded that Satan be gone in Jesus' name. He prayed and asked Jesus Christ to forgive him, to come into his life, and to be his Lord and Savior. He was set free. This man told me stories about Satan and his demons and what they did to him, how doors and windows would just open in his house. He told of the great torment that he experienced from the demons. He talked about how they afflicted him with physical, emotional pain, and mental pain. He said after the pastor had prayed for him, it intensified more than sevenfold.

This man got a job driving an eighteen-wheeler. He was in our church for approximately three months and then was transferred to Houston. Every Christmas, for years, I received a thank-you note from him for not praying for him when he came to my office the first time but waiting until he was ready to come to Christ. With each letter, he told me of the joy and the victory of serving Jesus.

Matthew 12:43–45 says:

> When the unclean spirit is gone out of a man, he walketh through dry places, seeking rest, and findeth none. Then he saith, I will return into my house from whence I came out; and when he is come, he findeth it empty, swept, and garnished. Then goeth he, and taketh with himself seven other spirits more wicked than himself, and they enter in and dwell there: and the last state of that man is worse than the first. Even so shall it be also unto this wicked generation.

The Scripture tells us what happens if the demons are cast out and the house is not filled. The only way the house can be filled is by receiving Jesus Christ. The spirits will go out, and they will find seven worse spirits and bring them back with them. When they find the house empty and clean, they will come in and repossess the house. The second state will be far worse than the first. You should never pray for a person to be delivered from demon-possession until that person, through the Word of God, comes to know that they are demon-possessed. That person must be seeking God. When the man in the cemetery that was demon-possessed saw Jesus, he came to him and worshipped him.

Mark 5:1–20 says:

> And they came over unto the other side of the sea, into the country of the Gadarenes. And when he was come out of the ship, immediately there met him out of the tombs a man with an unclean spirit, Who had his dwelling among the tombs; and no man could bind him, no, not with chains: Because that he had been often bound with fetters and chains, and the chains had been plucked asunder by him, and the fetters broken in pieces: neither could any man tame him. And always, night and day, he was in the mountains, and in the tombs, crying, and cutting himself with stones. But when he saw Jesus afar off, he ran and worshipped him, And cried with a loud voice, and said, What have I to do with thee, Jesus, thou Son of the most high God? I adjure thee by God, that thou torment me not. For he said unto him, Come out of the man, thou unclean spirit. And he asked him, What is thy name? And he answered, saying, My name is Legion: for we are many. And he besought him much that he would not send them away out of the country. Now there was there nigh unto the mountains a great herd of swine feeding. And all the

devils besought him, saying, Send us into the swine, that we may enter into them. And forthwith Jesus gave them leave. And the unclean spirits went out, and entered into the swine: and the herd ran violently down a steep place into the sea, (they were about two thousand) and were choked in the sea. And they that fed the swine fled, and told it in the city, and in the country. And they went out to see what it was that was done. And they come to Jesus, and see him that was possessed with the devil, and had the legion, sitting, and clothed, and in his right mind: and they were afraid. And they that saw it told them how it befell to him that was possessed with the devil, and also concerning the swine. And they began to pray him to depart out of their coasts. And when he was come into the ship, he that had been possessed with the devil prayed him that he might be with him. Howbeit Jesus suffered him not, but saith unto him, Go home to thy friends, and tell them how great things the Lord hath done for thee, and hath had compassion on thee. And he departed, and began to publish in Decapolis how great things Jesus had done for him: and all men did marvel.

MINISTER OF RIGHTEOUSNESS

Before I became a pastor, we were attending a church in which the pastor had asked me to help him minister at the altars. One morning, after the service, when the altar call was given, there was a man that came to the altars who wanted to pray for others. God spoke to me and told me that he was a minister of righteousness. I started to visit with the man and found that he had been a drug addict. After several years of doing cocaine and heroin, he reached his end. He decided to overdose to end the misery and his life.

While he was fading out, an angel of light appeared to him and told him that he was Jesus and that if he would serve him, he would save his life. So the man agreed to it, and he did not die. Then he became a minister of righteousness, traveling as an evangelist, teaching self-righteousness and works, and preaching in churches. He was telling the story of how Jesus had saved him from a drug overdose and of being set free from drugs.

I thought, *Lord, you said that this man is a minister of righteousness*. I asked the man to confess Jesus Christ has come in the flesh.

The demon spoke and said, "We do not serve that God."

So then I asked the man if he had peace, and he said, "No, I am tormented day and night."

I opened the Scriptures and showed the man that Jesus came to give us peace. After the Word had discerned that he did not have peace and that he had not met Jesus Christ but had met the angel of light, he realized that he was demon-possessed and needed deliverance. He was delivered and received Jesus Christ.

Second Corinthians 11:13–15 says:

> For such are false apostles, deceitful workers, transforming themselves into the apostles of Christ. And no marvel; for Satan himself is transformed into an angel of light. Therefore it is no great thing if his ministers also be transformed as the ministers of righteousness; whose end shall be according to their works.

That is no marvel, for Satan himself is transformed into an angel of light; therefore it is no great thing if his ministers also be transformed as ministers of righteousness whose end shall be according to their works. I have met at least seven men, all with similar stories. While on a trip with drugs, the angel of light came to them, offering to save them if they would serve him, and they became ministers of righteousness. They were all traveling around, preaching in churches. And the sad thing is that pastors would hear their testimony of how they were delivered from drugs and an overdose and allow them to teach and preach in their churches. The pastors had no discernment.

FALSE PROPHETS

I pastored a church called Mount Zion Fellowship. It was in the Oak Lawn area of Dallas, Texas. When we started the church, the area was made up of primarily drug addicts, hippies, and prostitutes. As these people received Christ and their lives got straightened out, they started marrying and starting families. The church became a young family church. Then the homosexuals moved into the Oak Lawn area, and it became predominantly a homosexual community. We reached out to the homosexuals to try to bring them to Christ. We sent out a track to the 75219 zip code. That created no small controversy, but it did put us on the map. We became known as the church in the homosexual community with an outreach to homosexuals.

One day I received a telephone call from a man who had a Christian television station. He called me because he wanted me to come to the station and meet a man from California that had a ministry for homosexuals. This man had been in the Dallas-Fort Worth area for several weeks, preaching in many of the very large churches—Baptist,

Presbyterian, Assembly of God, and independent charismatic churches.

I went to the television station, and when I arrived, I met the man. God spoke to me and told me that he was a false prophet. I began to ask him questions about his salvation, how he had become saved, and how he knew that he was saved. He seemed to have all the right answers. Second Corinthians 11:13–15 describes false apostles and deceitful workers who transform themselves into the apostles of Christ. I asked him if he was tormented, and he told me that he was tormented day and night. I told him that the true Jesus, the Son of God, gave peace. He said that he did not have the peace that I was talking about. Then, when I questioned him further, I found out that he was still living with his homosexual partner and had not changed.

I asked him if he would like to have peace and receive Jesus Christ as his Lord and Savior. He told me that he was not interested in changing his lifestyle. I told him that I would expose him for who he was and what he was. His response was, "I knew this was coming. Do what you must do." I exposed him.

DEMONS AND CHRISTIANS

There was a man who came into my office; he looked like death warmed over. He had been up for over sixty hours without any sleep while in demon deliverance. A group of people was casting all these demons out of him. He had been vomiting and coughing for sixty hours. The man was in such a state that he barely knew his own name. I first ministered to his physical needs by getting some fluids in him, getting him rehydrated, and giving him some nutrition.

First Corinthians 12:3 says:

> Wherefore I give you to understand, that no man speaking by the Spirit of God calleth Jesus accursed: and that no man can say that Jesus is the Lord, but by the Holy Ghost.

No man can call Jesus Lord, except by the Holy Ghost.

First Corinthians 3:11–12 says:

> For other foundation can no man lay than that is laid, which is Jesus Christ. Now if any man build upon this foundation gold, silver, precious stones, wood, hay, stubble.

There is only one foundation that could be laid, and that is Jesus Christ. I have discovered if you ask a man or woman where Jesus is in relationship to them, if they are not truly born again, they cannot say that Jesus is in their heart. If you ask people that are not saved this question, usually they will say, "Well, he is around me or is near me or I want him." But a born-again believer will confess that Jesus Christ has come into their heart.

So I asked this young man where Jesus was in relation to him. He said, "He's in my heart." The Scripture says that greater is he that is in you than he that is in the world. Jesus said a house divided against itself cannot stand. As a born-again believer, you cannot have demons in your spirit. He then asked why he was vomiting and coughing and spitting out these demons. I told him that if you yield yourself to Satan, he will manifest himself and that if it were possible, he would deceive you. He asked God to forgive him for his unbelief. He thanked the Lord for his salvation, and he was free.

I was at church one night, ministering at the altar. A lady that had gone to the altar week after week for several months was there. The pastor came to me, and he asked if I would please minister to this lady. I went to the lady, and

God spoke to me and said that she was demon-possessed. I asked her where Jesus was in relationship to her, and she said, "All around me."

I asked her if she had peace, and she replied that she did not have peace. I asked her if she wanted to know where Jesus was in relation to her, and she replied, "Yes." She prayed and received Jesus Christ as her Lord and Savior. Then upon further questioning, I discovered that she had been in one of the demon deliverance ministries that said Christians could have a demon in them. On a weekly basis, she had been going through deliverance. Because of her horrendous lifestyle, she truly had demons that came out of her. But she was not born again at that time.

I was involved in a ministry in which the directors of the ministry were promoting the demon deliverance of Christians. They gave me six tapes by Derek Prince. I'd listen to the tapes, and they were so right on scripturally. I thought, God, I know that this is not right, but I cannot find error in the Scripture.

God told me to listen again, and he would show me the error, so I listened again. The woman that this entire doctrine was based upon was similar to the woman I had just dealt with. They had asked her if she was a Christian, and she said she was a Christian. But they had not ascertained that she was truly born again, and she was not born again. So they were casting demons out of this woman, believing she was saved when she was not. Most false doctrine is derived from experience. If the experience lines up with the Scripture, then it is true. But you cannot make a doctrine out of an experience.

TESTING THE SPIRITS

First John 1:1 says:

> Beloved, believe not every spirit, but
> try the spirits whether they are of God:
> because many false prophets are gone out
> into the world.

God tells us to test the spirits to be sure they are of God. He tells us that every spirit that does not confess Jesus Christ is come in the flesh is not of God. This Scripture troubled me for years as I tried to figure out how a spirit would confess Jesus Christ come in the flesh.

Philippians 2:5–11 says:

> Let this mind be in you, which was
> also in Christ Jesus: Who, being in the
> form of God, thought it not robbery to be
> equal with God: But made himself of no
> reputation, and took upon him the form
> of a servant, and was made in the likeness

of men: And being found in fashion as a man, he humbled himself, and became obedient unto death, even the death of the cross. Wherefore God also hath highly exalted him, and given him a name which is above every name: That at the name of Jesus every knee should bow, of things in heaven, and things in earth, and things under the earth; And that every tongue should confess that Jesus Christ is Lord, to the glory of God the Father.

God put the deity of Jesus in a blind trust, and Jesus became the Son of Man. Jesus Christ is God. But when Jesus became the Son of Man, he essentially gave up his Godship. He came to show us how to live for God. Jesus did not make himself a reputation but humbled himself, became a servant, and went to the cross. The sole purpose of Jesus in his first coming was to go to the cross. Jesus said that he did not do any works unless they were his Father's works and would glorify his Father. Jesus did not come to glorify himself but rather his Father. Jesus' purpose was to go to the cross so that sinful flesh might die on the cross.

Matthew 16:24–27 says:

Then said Jesus unto his disciples, If any man will come after me, let him deny himself, and take up his cross, and follow me. For whosoever will save his life shall lose it: and whosoever will lose his life for my sake shall find it. For what is a man profited, if he shall gain the whole world, and lose his own soul? or what shall a man give in exchange for his soul? For the Son of man shall come in the glory of his Father with his angels; and then he shall reward every man according to his works.

Jesus tells us to take up our cross, deny ourselves, and follow him. So we find that when our spirit is asked to confess Jesus Christ come in the flesh, that spirit should do nothing to glorify ourselves. Jesus said that he came to do his Father's works and that he did no works unless they were his Father's. He said that he spoke only the words that his Father gave him.

Matthew 7:21–23 says:

> Not every one that saith unto me, Lord, Lord, shall enter into the kingdom of heaven; but he that doeth the will of my Father which is in heaven. Many will say to me in that day, Lord, Lord, have we not prophesied in thy name? and in thy name have cast out devils? and in thy name done many wonderful works? And then will I profess unto them, I never knew you: depart from me, ye that work iniquity.

Not everyone that says, "Lord, Lord" shall enter into the kingdom of heaven but those that do the works of the Father. He said that many will say that they have prophesied in his name, done many wonderful works in his name, cast out demons in his name, and he will say unto them depart from me you workers of iniquity. There is a grave danger that when we start walking with God and God starts using us to perform miracles, we begin to believe that we are God's man of the hour and God's man of power. We start to believe the press. Pride enters our lives. It becomes very subtle that we are saying we only want to glorify God, but we are seeking self-glory.

I met a man that said God had anointed his hands, and if he touched people, they would be healed. He insisted that for people to be healed, he must touch them and pray for them. I don't know about you, but this scares me to death. Because he said it was his touch that brought the healing, it brought glory and honor to him, even though he was saying he was giving God the glory.

Matthew 7:15–20 says:

> Beware of false prophets, which come to you in sheep's clothing, but inwardly they are ravening wolves. Ye shall know them by their fruits. Do men gather grapes of thorns, or figs of thistles? Even so every good tree bringeth forth good fruit; but a corrupt tree bringeth forth evil fruit. A good tree cannot bring forth evil fruit, neither can a corrupt tree bring

forth good fruit. Every tree that bringeth not forth good fruit is hewn down, and cast into the fire. Wherefore by their fruits ye shall know them.

God cautioned us to beware of false prophets that come to us in sheep's clothing but inwardly are raving wolves. He says we shall know them by their fruit. Does their fruit bring self-glory? Or does it glorify God?

Romans 12:3 says:

For I say, through the grace given unto me, to every man that is among you, not to think of himself more highly than he ought to think; but to think soberly, according as God hath dealt to every man the measure of faith.

That measure of faith is enough faith to pray and receive Jesus Christ as our Lord and Savior.

Ephesians 2:8–9 says:

For by grace are ye saved through faith; and that not of yourselves: it is the gift of God: Not of works, lest any man should boast.

God tells us that we are saved by grace through faith and that faith is a gift from God. We do not have enough faith to believe in God for salvation if he has not given it to us.

Matthew 13:11–17 says:

> He answered and said unto them, Because it is given unto you to know the mysteries of the kingdom of heaven, but to them it is not given. For whosoever hath, to him shall be given, and he shall have more abundance: but whosoever hath not, from him shall be taken away even that he hath. Therefore speak I to them in parables: because they seeing see not; and hearing they hear not, neither do they understand. And in them is fulfilled the prophecy of Esaias, which saith, By hearing ye shall hear, and shall not understand; and seeing ye shall see, and shall not perceive: For this people's heart is waxed gross, and their ears are dull of hearing, and their eyes they have closed; lest at any time they should see with their eyes, and hear with their ears, and should understand with their heart, and should be converted, and I should heal them. But blessed are your eyes, for they see: and your ears, for they hear. For verily I say unto you, That many prophets and righteous men have desired to see those things which ye see, and have not seen them; and

to hear those things which ye hear, and have not heard them.

Romans 10:17 says:

So then faith cometh by hearing, and hearing by the word of God.

Faith comes by hearing and hearing by the Word of God. Before we came to Christ, our spirit was dead. The Word says "The dead shall hear my voice and be made alive." John 6:44–45 says:

No man can come to me, except the Father which hath sent me draw him: and I will raise him up at the last day. It is written in the prophets, And they shall be all taught of God. Every man therefore that hath heard, and hath learned of the Father, cometh unto me.

The Word tells us that we did not come to the Father on our own, but he drew us. Then it tells us that everyone that is taught of God and has heard and learned of God will come to him. It becomes important that we realize how precious that gift of faith is. In Matthew 13, they had spiritual ears but had closed them, and thus they could not hear the faith. And God says that those that do not apply works to their faith and believe in him, he will take the faith that they have.

FAITH AND WORKS

James 2:14–26 says:

> What doth it profit, my brethren,
> though a man say he hath faith, and
> have not works? can faith save him? If a
> brother or sister be naked, and destitute
> of daily food, And one of you say unto
> them, Depart in peace, be ye warmed
> and filled; notwithstanding ye give them
> not those things which are needful to the
> body; what doth it profit? Even so faith,
> if it hath not works, is dead, being alone.
> Yea, a man may say, Thou hast faith, and
> I have works: shew me thy faith without
> thy works, and I will shew thee my faith
> by my works. Thou believest that there is
> one God; thou doest well: the devils also
> believe, and tremble. But wilt thou know,
> O vain man, that faith without works is
> dead? Was not Abraham our father justi-

fied by works, when he had offered Isaac his son upon the altar? Seest thou how faith wrought with his works, and by works was faith made perfect? And the scripture was fulfilled which saith, Abraham believed God, and it was imputed unto him for righteousness: and he was called the Friend of God. Ye see then how that by works a man is justified, and not by faith only. Likewise also was not Rahab the harlot justified by works, when she had received the messengers, and had sent them out another way? For as the body without the spirit is dead, so faith without works is dead also.

God tells us that Abraham's faith was made complete by his works when he offered Isaac upon the altar. Abraham believed that God could raise Isaac up from the ashes and that he might be his heir. It says that Rahab was justified by her works when she had received the messengers and sent them out another way. The body without the spirit is dead, so faith without works is dead also.

Romans 10:8–13 says:

But what saith it? The word is nigh thee, even in thy mouth, and in thy heart: that is, the word of faith, which we preach; That if thou shalt confess with thy mouth the Lord Jesus, and shalt believe in thine heart that God hath raised him from the dead, thou shalt be saved. For with the heart man believeth unto righteousness; and with the mouth confession is made unto salvation. For the scripture saith, Whosoever believeth on him shall not be ashamed. For there is no difference between the Jew and the Greek: for the same Lord over all is rich unto all that call upon him. For whosoever shall call upon the name of the Lord shall be saved.

Many times, we quote Romans 10:9–10 and 13, and we leave out verse 8. This verse tells us that the Word is very near us, even in our mouth, in our heart, and is the Word of faith that we need to profess Christ. A powerful example of works applied to faith is when we came to Christ. It tells us if we will confess the Lord Jesus Christ and shall believe in our hearts that God raised him from the dead, we shall be saved. Then the next verse comes back and tells us that with the heart, we believe unto righteousness, and with the mouth, confession is made unto salvation. What it is saying is if we believe that God raised Jesus Christ from the dead and we will confess this with our mouth, we have applied the work of faith to the Word that whosoever shall call on the name of the Lord shall be saved. We will be saved and we are saved.

John 6:28–29 says:

> Then said they unto him, What shall
> we do, that we might work the works of
> God? Jesus answered and said unto them,
> This is the work of God, that ye believe on
> him whom he hath sent.

The disciples asked what they should do to do the works of God. Jesus told them that the works of God are to believe in him who God sent.

If I should hear the Scripture, "You shall lay hands on the sick and they shall recover" and if I lay my hands on the sick person and pray for them, God will heal them. Also, if I have faith that God will deliver and pray for a demon deliverance, God will free that person from demon possession. This is applying works to faith which is heard from the Word of God. I will relate a true story that happened in the church that I was pastoring. There was a man and woman that would come into the service after it had started and would leave just as the invitation was given. They did not want to talk to anyone. They would come for several weeks. Then they would be gone for a while, and they would come back again.

This repeated for approximately a year. One Sunday morning as I was preaching, I received a word from the Lord that there was someone in the congregation that had cancer and if they would come forward for prayer, God would heal them. And I knew in my spirit that it was this man. The man did not come forward, but he and his wife left. About three months later, the man and his wife came back to the church, and his hand had been amputated. He waited until after the service was over and came up to talk to me. He said I was in the church when the word was given that if someone that had cancer would come forward and receive prayer, they would be healed. He said, "I was that person. I did not come, and because of the cancer in my hand, I had to have my hand amputated. You probably wonder why I did not come forward. You were a nobody. I had gone all over the United States to be prayed for by the great healers. I went to Catherine Kuhlman, Kenneth Hagan, Oral Roberts, and many others. I was not healed when these people prayed for me, and why would I think it would be any different with a nobody?" Then with tears in his eyes, he said, "Because of my pride, I lost my hand. God showed me that it was him, that God was the healer, not the man or woman that prayed for them." Here is a good example in which faith without works is dead. When God speaks faith, a person needs to apply works to the faith whether it is for salvation, healing, demon deliverance, or any other aspect of their walk with God.

ABOUT THE AUTHOR

The author, Dr. Ernest S. Martin, grew up on a large ranch in North Dakota where his family had a dairy and raised both commercial and registered Herefords. They grew wheat, durum, barley, oats, and alfalfa hay. Growing up on a farm and ranch gave Ernest insight into the Scriptures as many illustrations in the Word of God are related to sheep, goats, and growing grain.

While in high school, Ernest studied a curriculum geared to be an engineer but changed to veterinary medicine at North Dakota State University. He received his DVM from Oklahoma State University. While doing post-doctoral research at OSU, he met his wife, Jan, who was doing graduate work in chemistry. They were married eleven weeks later in 1966.

After moving to Dallas, Texas, Ernest eventually had his own animal hospital. He received Jesus as his Savior on August 21, 1970, and soon started an outreach Bible study for hippies. This outreach became a church that Ernest pastored while still practicing veterinary medicine. After selling his veterinary practice at age sixty-two, he went to firefighter school and became a volunteer firefighter, and he is currently the chaplain of the Melissa Fire Department. Ernest and his wife, Jan, have four sons, five granddaughters, and one grandson.

Printed in the USA
CPSIA information can be obtained
at www.ICGtesting.com
JSHW081747031223
52887JS00002B/71

9 798887 518701